On The Shoulders of My Shepherd

Lessons on How to Heal Before Marriage

Amaris L. Martin

ON THE SHOULDERS OF MY SHEPHERD

On the Shoulders of My Shepherd

Lessons on How to Heal Before Marriage ©
by Amaris L. Martin

ISBN-13: 978-0692678732 (Queendom Come Publishing)
ISBN-10: 0692678735
First Print April 2016
10 9 8 7 6 5 4 3 2 1

Copyright © 2016 by Queendom Come Publishing
LIBRARY OF CONGRESS CATALOGING IN PUBLICATION
Queendom Come Publishing
www.queendomcomecoaching.com

PUBLISHER'S NOTE

This book is based on a true story. Names, characters, places, and incidents are real. Any resemblance to actual persons, living or dead, business establishments, or locales have been changed to protect those involved.

All Scripture quotations, unless otherwise indicated, are taken from the Holy Bible, New International Version®, NIV®. Copyright ©1973, 1978, 1984, 2011 by Biblica, Inc.™ Used by permission of Zondervan. All rights reserved worldwide. www.zondervan.com The "NIV" and "New International Version" are trademarks registered in the United States Patent and Trademark Office by Biblica, Inc.™

ON THE SHOULDERS OF MY SHEPHERD

Dedication

This book is dedicated to my beloved grandparents, LB and Nora McWhorter.

Your love for God and one another painted a picture of unconditional love and commitment that inspired my heart to believe in righteous love. Your marriage gave me hope and inspiration. Thank you for the lessons you taught, unbeknownst to you, that shaped my life. I am indebted for the ways you made loving look easy, adventurous and beautiful...

To the little boy who taught me how to love: my son, Elijah. This book also belongs to you. You have been my greatest gift. Everything about you makes me want to learn to love better. Mommy loves you...

ON THE SHOULDERS OF MY SHEPHERD

On The Shoulders of My Shepherd

Lessons on How to Heal Before Marriage

Amaris L. Martin

ON THE SHOULDERS OF MY SHEPHERD

Contents

Foreword by Tanika Dillard

Preface 16

Chapter 1: Our Need for Acceptance...............................30

Chapter 2: The Dilution Factor 38

Chapter 3: Parrot Talk 46

Chapter 4: Verbally Transmitted Disease 54

Chapter 5: Replacing Misplaced Expectations 60

Chapter 6: Performance Driven Life 70

Chapter 7: The Pursuit of Righteousness 92

Epilogue...100

Acknowledgements 104

About the Author 108

ON THE SHOULDERS OF MY SHEPHERD

Foreword

By Tanika Dillard, author of Building a Family Breaks My Heart

As a former singles ministry participant and leader, I vividly recall the depth of my desire for relationship and marriage. I silently observed those wives who, in my opinion, did marriage well and made their actions my standard. I have listened to countless stories of failed relationships, utter heartbreak and "happily ever afters". The reverberating theme in conversations from singles reflected their longing for true love.

On the Shoulders of My Shepherd is a genuine invitation to the most cherished love through intentional encounters with God. Amaris has used her life experiences as a tool to empower others to pursue healing. Each chapter is eloquently created to identify the common challenges, thinking, and behaviors of single individuals.   Readers are continuously redirected to the Shepherd.

I recommend this literary jewel to anyone who is ready to abandon unproductive thinking and relationships. The truth found within these pages, when appropriately applied, will produce whole, complete singles who live out their greatest love story; not in the arms of another man or woman but On the Shoulders of the Shepherd.

Tanika Dillard

"He tends his flock like a shepherd:

He gathers the lambs in his arms

and carries them close to his heart" Isaiah 40:11

ON THE SHOULDERS OF MY SHEPHERD

Preface

If you've picked up this book, chances are you have had your fair share of disappointments in relationships. I am willing to bet that your heart has been broken a time or two, and you decided to carry the pieces of your broken heart in one hand and pick up this book with the other. First, let me encourage you by saying you're not alone on Heartbreak Island. Every heart, male and female alike, has drifted on the shores of brokenness; most of us on rotting driftwood, barely alive, thirsty, starving, exhausted, sunburned, and delusional. Don't be fooled. No one is exempt from reenacting a scene of Tom Hanks' character in the movie Cast Away. You remember the story of the ship wrecked Chuck whose only friend was a soccer ball, Wilson. He was stranded on an island without hopes of rescue. We've all been washed up by love, or at least what we thought was love. So rather than opening these pages and wading in a pool of regret and guilt, know that we all have been there. Heartbreak is not discriminatory. It has been intimate with each of us, and for some of us, it has been an off again-on again partner. While heartbreak is a commonplace, sadly healing is not. The epidemic of entering toxic, unhealthy relationships guarantees brokenness and leaves a trail of victims. Yet, often times we leave those relationships brutally victimized only to become victimizers. We either consciously or sometimes subconsciously take on the behaviors of the last person who hurt us. You've heard the colloquial phrase, "Hurt people, hurt people. Thus, the cycle continues, creating communities that thrive on hurt, abuse, mistrust and misrepresentation.

This purpose of this book is to serve as an antidote for carrying wounds from relationship to relationship and re-infecting others. The goal is to present an uncommon, yet critical approach to ending the vicious cycle of brokenness and begin healing before we commit to the next relationship. Your own life will be the focus of this book. Not your last partner or friend, but you. This will be your journey. Make yourself your focus as you turn these pages. It is so tempting to place blame on those who hurt us. However, the painful truth is, we willingly walked through the doors of the relationship. We chose our inflictors. We decided...we acquiesced...we pursued...we leaped...it was us. Personal responsibility is often a bitter pill to ingest. But rather than inflict more pain on ourselves, let's begin to examine the underlying, neglected roots that led to our decisions.

Let me begin by congratulating you on choosing to break the gambit of heartbreak and instead walk the path of convalescence. There are few who chose this path because of the work it requires, yet I encourage you to stay on course. Current divorce rates are a prime example of how many chose the wider road of unforgiveness, bitterness and low self-worth while entering marriage. I'm sure if you could ask any married woman or man who neglected the hard self-work prior to marriage, they would encourage you to do otherwise. They'd tell you to take the narrow path to becoming whole. Choose the straight path. Choose to heal.

Enter through the narrow gate; for the gate is wide and the way is broad that leads to destruction, and there are many who enter through it. Matthew 7:13 NASB

ON THE SHOULDERS OF MY SHEPHERD

When I began writing this book, I was tempted to develop a generic "12-Step Program" or write a curriculum on "How to Heal in 8 weeks", but truthfully there can be no time restraints placed on healing. There is no magical, proven time table on how to heal. Healing is a process that has a mind of its own. It simply takes time. That's it. No secret formula. No easy 3- step, clap your hands, jump up and down while spinning tricks. It's putting in the hard work, while offering yourself honesty, patience and grace. Your healing works at the rate you are willing to address you!

Not only does healing take time, it also takes a great level of persistence. I wish I could guarantee that after one round of addressing your relational wounds, you would be "fixed", but chances are, addressing one wound may only give leeway to expose more wounds. Trust the process anyhow; I can guarantee you that it's worth finishing.

One other guarantee I can give you is that you will not be alone on this journey to healing and wholeness. You have been given a Guide on the path to becoming aware of your wounds, how to heal and how to avoid future self-inflicted scars. There is One who will carry you on this new terrain. Remember, pain has become an all too familiar dwelling place for us, so we are in need of someone who will take us into unfamiliar territory, without inflicting any further harm on us. We are in need of a Shepherd.

"The Lord is my Shepherd....He guides me along the right paths for his name's sake." Psalms 23:1, 3

By nature, I believe we are very nomadic people. Settling or standing still is hard for us. We find being stationary very difficult. Have you ever observed kindergarten aged boys in a classroom? They are fidgety and antsy, eagerly waiting to move to the next center. We aren't much different in our relationships as adults. We become easily distracted and led astray by tantalizing desires, thus we jump from relationship to relationship, hoping this next one will satisfy our "needs". God already knew our wandering tendency, that's why He sent us a Shepherd. He knew we would need an escort to get back on the right path in not only relationships, but life itself.

There has been numerous sermons and blogs composed about the relationship between a shepherd and his flock. It's no wonder.

Sheep are mentioned more than 500 times in the Bible. Sheep were often symbolic of God's chosen people. Even Jesus was referred to as the "Lamb of God". There are countless other references to sheep and shepherds in the Bible, including King David, the little shepherd boy. There are so many great scriptural lessons that can be drawn from tales of the lives of sheep and shepherds. There's a story that most resembled the path I walked with God as he prepared me for marriage. It was a story of how the shepherd would break the legs of his sheep to keep them safe from their own destructive tendencies. Before you tune me out or call PETA (People for the Ethical Treatment of Animals), hear my personal testimony of why this story struck a nerve (or old wound). The story begins with a disobedient sheep. It was the sheep who was chronically led away from his flock because of the temptations outside the shepherd's reach. It is also the story of the difficult decision of a loving shepherd who wanted the best for his flock. It starts here.

Sheep's innate mantra is 'there is safety in numbers'. By nature, sheep are followers and stick together in tightly packed flocks. Rightfully so, there are wolves, coyotes, foxes and other predators out there-hungry for the taste of lamb chops! So yes, any smart sheep knows to stick with their flock in order to survive. Lucky for them, they didn't have to rely on the safety of the flock alone. Each flock had their own shepherd. The shepherd was responsible for leading the sheep and protecting them from pending danger. Sheep aren't dumb creatures; they can recognize the faces of their sheep counterparts and even the face of their shepherd. Even more so, they recognize their shepherd's voice. And more than just his voice, sheep understood the tone of his voice. This relationship wasn't one sided either. Shepherds were well acquainted with their sheep too, even naming each of them and sensing their presence. A good shepherd would know if even one of his sheep were missing and would diligently search for the one.

Can we pause on the sheep lesson for a moment to ask this question? How many times has God had to come looking for you? While you were in arms of Mr. or Mrs. Wrong, how frantically did He have to hunt for you? I know that fine man seemed perfect, right? He had charisma, the degree, the car, the wardrobe and an ego to match. He had your nose so wide open; you didn't even realize you had walked away from the Shepherd. It's okay. Don't let guilt make you shut this book. I love you too much to attempt to condemn you. Each of us has been lost in the wrong relationships: lovers, friends, jobs, careers, churches…we've all lost sight of our compass and landed in the den of wolves. This is the perfect place to give you good news though.....He will look for you!

"Suppose one of you has a hundred sheep and loses one of them. Doesn't he leave the ninety-nine in the open country and go after the lost sheep until he finds it? And when he finds it, he joyfully puts it on his shoulders and goes home." Luke 15:4 NIV

Your Shepherd will come for you. He's coming for you now. He loved you enough to never leave you in the place you wandered off to… He will come find you and carry you back on His shoulders. Now, that we've established that reminder, let's get back to our sheep.

While traveling across rugged countryside, sheep not only listened for the voice of their shepherd, but they looked for his staff. His staff was often used to protect them from predators. But when dealing with stubborn sheep, the staff was also used for correction. If a sheep would wander away from the flock, the shepherd would use the staff's crook to redirect the sheep by its neck. However, in the case that a sheep consistently veered away from the flock into danger, despite previous warnings, the staff's crook was used to break the sheep's legs to prevent him from being hurt or killed outside the safety of the flock. Once done, the shepherd would set the broken limb and carry the wounded sheep on his shoulders for the remainder of the journey. While on the shepherd's shoulder, the sheep was completely dependent on the shepherd for everything. In the time the sheep spent on the shepherd's shoulders, his relationship deepened. You see, during this very intimate time, the sheep learned how to trust his shepherd. I imagine that wounded sheep had privy to secret conversations with the shepherd-conversations offering explanations about why he made the hard decision to break his legs...conversations about the benefits of remaining near the shepherd, about what the future would hold and about all the great things the sheep would do after he healed. I can imagine that because this is what my time of healing felt like for me. It was a time when I felt like He and I were all alone in our own world. I began to receive clarity on all the times He had gently warned me before…the times He tried to protect me from heartbreak, but I chose to ignore His voice. There were intimate walks where He declared His love for me and how much He wanted to do in my life. It was on those cold nights, where my wounds began to ache, that He nursed me until the pain ceased. Early some mornings, He'd wake me up before dawn, just to share the plans He had for me. He was relentless in showering me with love, exhorting my worth and value. He whispered secrets in my ear. I loved those days, nestled so close to Him that I could hear His breathing. I loved those days so much, that on the day He placed me back in the fields, I was determined to never leave His side again. That was my shoulder experience. That is the enclosure of these pages that I wish to share with you.

Some theologians argue that the story of shepherds breaking the legs of their sheep is an absolute myth. It is not my intent to turn this book into a theological debate. You will find theologians on either side who will debate the validity of this reference. It will always be my goal to present biblically sound material. I dare not misrepresent the Word of God. However, in studying this topic and finding no concrete evidence of this practice, I have decided to use this story as a parable accompanied by biblical principles. I decided to write about my own personal journey on the shoulders of a Shepherd who loved me enough to pull me away from my own destructive proclivities of settling for unhealthy relationships. I wanted to share the story of how I have traveled through valleys, mountain tops, deserts and plains, all the while being carried by a Master Guide. I cannot attest to the validity of sheep's legs being broken and mended by a shepherd, but I can bear witness to wandering into the dangerous terrain of low self-worth and poor relational choices and being broken, bound and then carried by Someone who knew I was worthy of more. I am grateful for the view from atop His shoulders. It's from that viewpoint that allowed me to birth this book. It is my prayer that you have your own shoulder experience and find healing. It is my deepest desire that you may find bits and pieces of your own story in these pages and be assured that you can be whole.

In the chapters that are to follow, we are going to address some of the possible root causes for our current state of being wounded. Please understand. It is not my intent to discount the actual act that hurt you. I dare not discount or dismiss your personal account of heartbreak. Did the last partner cheat on you? Did the last man you trusted lie to you? Or did the last woman you gave your heart to turn it into a doormat? Your answer may be "yes, absolutely!" Of course it happened. The deed was done. But if we allow our focus to rest on what was done to us, rather than allow our Shepherd to reveal the part we played, it will result in bitterness and blame. I trust by now, you've realized that the blame game is the worst conduit of healing. True healing and wholeness requires we take responsibility for our current condition by doing a root-cause analysis and examine ourselves.

It is here that I interject a disclaimer. The concepts or roots that we are about to delve into are simply my own personal scar repertoire. These chapters contain a very transparent view of the revelations I received as God healed me in preparation for healthier relationships. After a myriad of failed relationships and an inextinguishable desire for marriage, I caved in and asked God to prepare me as a wife. Unbeknownst to me, it would be a grueling journey of heart work and soul searching. This will be a journey of learning your Shepherd's voice and trusting Him to lead you. For me, that's when healing began to take place and maturity was no longer stagnant- the moment I trusted His voice. Before then, I wandered into wolf-filled pastures, despite the prodding of my Shepherd's staff. After nursing my wounds, limping back and slapping a Band-Aid on, I would develop amnesia or be lured off by what appeared to be a less threatening wolf pack, only to be wounded again. That's when I needed rescuing. I needed to be broken-broken enough to never want to leave my Shepherd's side and follow Him into wealthy, safe and abundant pastures.

I welcome you on a journey through the countryside of healing. We are about to embark on a voyage with a destination of wholeness. I know it's scary. Trust me. I've faced that same fear. Yet, trust me in this, the peace that accompanies being whole is worth every fearful step. Thank you for choosing you. Thank you for deciding to rest on His shoulders, while He heals you. I am excited about the revelation He will give you as we travel through these pages. Let's begin.

ON THE SHOULDERS OF MY SHEPHERD

Chapter One

Our Need for Acceptance

I am one of those people who love to sit in public places and people watch. It's absolutely fascinating. People intrigue me with their mannerisms, conversations, banter and the blended melodies of diverse walks of life. When I sit and people-watch, I am in absolute awe of the way God designed people. I am amazed at the creative mind of God, who over time has created innumerable human lives, each with unique characteristics, both physically and emotionally. It is hard to believe that there is not one single person in existence that has identical traits. Each one of us is different, all made by a masterminded God who designed every detail about our beings. That blows my mind. God is truly a creative genius. He took His time to handcraft each embryo in the womb of his mother, all the while, ensuring our individuality, even down to our fingerprints. In God's artistry of creating each of us differently, there are some parts of our emotional being that God made exactly the same. One of those emotional components is our need to be accepted by others.

Abraham Maslow, a humanist psychologist from the 1940's, caught wind of our need for acceptance, in addition to other basic needs. He suggested that all of our behaviors are motivated by our longing to fulfill certain needs. In theory, we are hardwired to do certain things in order to have our needs met. Maslow introduced his concept of what he called the *hierarchy of needs* in a paper entitled *A Theory of Human Motivation*. In his publication, Maslow taught that every person has an intrinsic propensity to fulfill five basic needs: physiological (air, food, clothing, shelter), safety (security and wellbeing), love or belonging (which I address as acceptance), esteem (the need for respect) and self-actualization (reaching your fullest potential). The meeting of all these needs is vital for both our survival and happiness. Rather than begin a psychology lesson, I want to focus on how our need for acceptance affects our relational choices and how failing to be aware of our insatiable need for it can be dangerous.

ON THE SHOULDERS OF MY SHEPHERD

There is a very important note you cannot afford to overlook about yourself and other people. We need to be loved and accepted by others. It's not a preference or a want even, it is an absolute need. We cannot survive without certain needs being met. You can only live a minimal number of days without food or water. If you travel in a harsh-weathered terrain for any length of time without the proper clothing or shelter, you can bet you won't survive

> *We need to be loved and accepted by others.*

long. Because we are aware of our need for food, clothing and shelter, we are less likely to neglect meeting those needs. Your grumbling stomach will refuse to stop quivering until you meet its need for food. Yet, we have a dangerous tendency to ignore how essential acceptance is for our survival. The need for acceptance drives so much of our behavior, however, we act in such an unconscious manner that we overlook how we are vying for a sense of belonging.

Do you ever wonder why in your younger years, you behaved in so many conflicting ways that you were sure you had multiple personalities? You constantly changed your behavior, your dialect, your wardrobe or even your preferences just to "fit in" to certain crowds. You became a social chameleon, blending into the norms of whomever you needed to impress. I say *you*, but I meant *us*. Yep, I'm included in the masses that succumb to social and societal pressures. I knew how to transform at the appropriate time, without any real effort and without anyone knowing they were in front of an imposter. I was a skilled counterfeit, a bamboozler and a slickster. If I was in church, I looked like an angelic church girl who knew how to raise my hands on cue. I had the church girl's stockings and slip. I knew the hymnal lyrics and would even rehearse with the choir. If you were looking for a Bible reading saint, I could fit the bill…but only while I was in a church setting. Don't get me wrong, this was not a fictional part of me. I loved God with my whole heart. I loved worship. I loved singing to Him. However, I knew it was acceptable at church, but not so cool in the classroom. So at school, you would not even recognize that same girl. Do you know how other students would look at me if I wore a slip and stockings to school and belt out "What a Friend We Have in Jesus"? Please!! I anticipated the joshing that waited if I appeared like a "Jesus freak" in school, so there I put on another front. I became cool. I talked like everyone else; dressed like everyone else; performed like everyone else. That's until I got home, where I had to meet the expectations of my parents. There's only one word that can describe how I ended each of my days of multiple personalities: exhausted.

If you have ever had to transform into many different personalities to please all the people in your life, I'm sure you can relate. It is a tremendous burden to pretend for others. This is true especially if you are constantly evolving due to immersion in multiple environments. At the end of the day, you often don't know who you really are. You have changed so much to meet the demands of others that you go to bed dizzy from all the dress changes. If you're not careful to manage all your multiple personalities, you slip up and present the wrong persona in the wrong environment: you'll wind up in the club shouting, "hallelujah"! It requires tiring work to always present your fake representative to people, who ultimately are changing themselves. Did you ever stop to question what was driving your multiple personality disorder? The driving force is the thing that Maslow discovered over 60 years ago: it's our need for acceptance.

Our need for acceptance will cause us to create a stellar production of "What Can I Do to Gain Your Love?" We will sometimes do regretful things just to have a sense of being loved, desired or simply accepted by people. All of us are guilty of doing things we'd rather forget to fit into the crowd or be wanted by one individual. That's how powerful this need is.

Here's where I want to make an important point, while you may feel embarrassed by your past acceptance-driven acts, please don't feel condemned. Our need for acceptance is a basic need, meaning we each have it. God is a relational God, who designed us to be in relationship with others. He made us to desire to be in

> *God is a relational God, who designed us to be in relationship with others*

relationships with people. He himself desires to be in a relationship with you. God proved how His intent was for us to want to relate and commune with others in Genesis 2:18.

"Then the LORD God said, "It is not good for the man to be alone; I will make him a helper suitable for him." NASB

ON THE SHOULDERS OF MY SHEPHERD

God never intended for us to be lone, self-sufficient beings. He designed our hearts and minds to need connection with people we have affection towards. For that reason, I believe our need to be accepted is God-inspired. Yet, because of the depth and abuse of that need, we have at times fallen into some unhealthy tendencies to meet it. However, since God designed the need, He also provided a means to heal from the shame of our attempts to be accepted by the wrong people. Your Shepherd wishes to reteach you about how your need to belong is an innate, survival-dependent longing that is meant to attach you to righteous relationships. The productivity and fulfillment of your life depends on connection to people. Don't repress your need to relate and bond. Allow your Shepherd to show you how to connect the right way: by giving your authentic self to others who are secure in their own authenticity. That's what righteous relationships are. They include people who know who they are and what they have to give while walking through life together. Only your Shepherd can tell you who you are and how to become righteous [who you were originally intended to be] (we will discuss this further in Chapter 7). He can teach you how to recognize other righteous individuals. I can attest to the freedom that comes from knowing your true self and feeling secure in giving that person to others. There is so much liberty in offering your authentic self to others. It takes away the work of pretending and removes the sting of fear of rejection. I can witness to the joys of connecting to people who really "get you"!! But you have to be willing to allow them to meet the *real* you.

I encourage you to listen intently as your Shepherd dispels the lies of past relational mistakes. There is a healthy way to meet your need. There are healthy people who can meet your need. There is a Guide who can lead into green pastures of genuine acceptance and love. You no longer need to pretend. Take off your mask and let Him lead you.

Chapter Two

The Dilution Factor

There's a phrase I have an extremely low tolerance for. As a matter of fact, it almost teeters on hatred. You've heard it, I'm sure. It's probably even been said about you. It's not age-specific. It's not geographically restricted. It's not gender-bias. Both men and women have been verbally assaulted by this five word phrase: "You think you're all that!!" Oh, what that small statement does to my blood pressure. I cringe at the mention of those words. Those words haunted me terribly during my middle school years. I was a small, petite girl with long hair and a love for learning, dance, stylish clothes and horses. I was so proud of my induction into the Beta Club and fresh clothes. I walked through the hallways, shy, but sure. That's until, I heard some girls whispering in the hallways: "she thinks she's all that.....she's so stuck up!" "What???? Stuck-up???"Of

36

course I didn't think I was "all that". What did I do to make them think that? I wondered if it was last week when I wore that plaid skirt with the pleats ....was that too much? Or maybe it was Tuesday when my mom let me wear my freshly pressed hair down and not in a ponytail? Or you know what; it probably was when Mrs. Jackson told me I did a great job on my test in front of the entire class? Yeah, that was it." This was my thought process and it was here where I began obsessing with other's opinion of me. I'm sure this was the onset of years of being too self-conscious and my self-worth took its first blow. I started a quest of people pleasing, just to end the whispering in the hallways. However, the whispers didn't subside, it only got louder and the people bolder. By my second year in middle school, the girls I tried so desperately to please stabbed me with a much bigger knife: "you must think you're white!!" At the time, there was no greater insult to me than being accused of denying the race of people I was so proud of belonging to. I couldn't be disassociated from the women and men I idolized-the great freedom fighters, civil rights leaders, inventors, educators and entertainers. No. This was the last draw. I had to do something. So, I denounced all I was and became what they said I should be. My grades dropped.

My attire downgraded. My hair was tucked away. My extracurricular

activities concluded. My membership to honors' societies was

revoked. I became someone new. I fell prey to what I like to call the

Dilution Factor. *The Dilution Factor* is simply the act of "watering"

yourself down in order

to gain acceptance.

When others appear

> *The Dilution Factor is simply the act of "watering" yourself down in order to gain acceptance*

intimated by our gifts, our skills or simply by our personality, we

discount ourselves rather than risk being isolated or ostracized. It is

ever so tempting to be who you think they need or want. In order to

fit into the crowd, we pretend and fake our authenticity, all the while

losing ourselves. We chose to play it small, rather than become the

BIG people God originally intended. One of my favorite quotes

sums it up perfectly:

"Our deepest fear is not that we are inadequate. Our deepest

fear is that we are powerful beyond measure. It is our light, not our

darkness that most frightens us. We ask ourselves, 'Who am I to be

brilliant, gorgeous, talented, fabulous?' Actually, who are you not to

be? You are a child of God. Your playing small does not serve the world. There is nothing enlightened about shrinking so that other people won't feel insecure around you. We are all meant to shine, as children do. We were born to make manifest the glory of God that is within us. It's not just in some of us; it's in everyone. And as we let our own light shine, we unconsciously give other people permission to do the same. As we are liberated from our own fear, our presence automatically liberates others."

— Marianne Williamson, a Return to Love: Reflections on the Principles of "A Course in Miracles"

The Dilution Factor becomes even more prevalent once we begin dating. Authenticity takes a back seat in the dating game. We replace our genuine selves with counterfeits in order to win the affections of a girl or guy. Our need to be impressive completely overrules the liberty that accompanies presenting our true selves. This is due to our need for acceptance (as mentioned in Chapter 1). We have such a deep need to be loved that we will become prototypes of the person we believe they want or need. Insecurities will convince us that if we give our most authentic selves in relationships, we will risk rejection. Rejection. Yes, that's really the root of our fear. We know all too well that the fear of rejection seems to project its voice through a megaphone-selling the lie that the real you won't be accepted, so your only option is to sell your fake representative.

Somewhere along our journey, we have been sold the lie that your true selves are unacceptable, unlovable, unattractive and unworthy. Why else would the last man or woman leave you, right? We form these hypotheses after heartbreak that misleads us into believing that something is wrong with us. So, in order to protect ourselves from the next one, we diminish the greatness inside of us, in hopes to gain the affection of another. Thus, a very potent individual becomes diluted by pretentiousness, mediocrity, uniformity and a facade. But haven't you realized how stifled you feel while withholding your true self? Have you not sensed the piercing pain of nonfulfillment while you lose more of you to become more like them? Aren't your tired of shelving your gifts, talents and interests while you perform on stage for a crowd who will never know the magnitude of your being. God intended for you to infiltrate the world by walking through this earth is His image.

Yet, you have let the world subject you to its osmosis and now there's no distinction between you and them. You've become murky. Your once concentrated, consecrated self has fallen prey to dilution.

Please don't feel alone here. Insecurities have gripped us all and at one point or another. The fear of rejection from the ones we love, respect or admire is a real thing. Our need to be accepted is hardwired in our brain, so don't dare feel condemned by succumbing to the *Dilution Factor*. Unbeknownst to you, your Shepherd knew your potency long before you even attempted to mask it. He knew the triggers that would make you deny your magnificence to blend in the crowd. But He also knew the point you'd reach in the pastures of complacency and mundanity. Your Shepherd knew your original design would begin to burst through the shell of the man/woman you constructed. He knew your gifts would break out because He's the one who deposited it there. Your Shepherd knew the kind of impact He needed you to make in this world and He gave you precisely what you needed to accomplish it. Pretending to be something you're not couldn't accomplish the grand plan He had for you. He needs you to go back to the original plan He had for your life. Trust me, it's not a plan of playing it small or shrinking or hiding. What He placed in you is much too big to minimize. Trying to fit all He placed in you in some mere people-pleasing mannequin will only make you feel constricted and uncomfortable. I encourage you to find quiet time alone with the Shepherd to allow Him to tell you all the reasons why He loves you. Do you know how much He loves to sing of His love for you (Zephaniah 3:17). I'm sure if you'd be His audience of one, He would tell you how fearfully and wonderfully made you are (Psalms 139:14). I'm willing to bet He'd tell you the plans He had to prosper you (Jeremiah 29:11). Your Shepherd desires to tell you just how special your gifts are and how they are meant to change the lives of people. You were never intended to water down the real you. It's here that your confidence begins to strengthen, because you finally believe what He says about you. It's your ah-ha moment. The very moment you begin to be engulfed by His love and your self-worth begins to grow. It is at this moment His love begins to melt the lie of worthlessness and you see your own reflection in Him. You begin to understand that the person under all those masks was made in the image of God Himself. Who would want to dilute Him? Don't reduce yourself for the approval of people who will never appreciate the greatness within you. You may have to come to the hurtful knowledge that not everyone was meant to be attached to you. Not everyone will be able to handle your life's assignment. That's okay. Don't run the risk of missing your highest potential by focusing on the wrong people. The right people will come along in time and you will recognize them by their acceptance, love and support. You will know them by the way they encourage you and even challenge you to shine. Those are the relationships worth waiting for. And while you're waiting, why not listen to the melody of your Shepherd who sings of the great works you will do together.

Do you hear him?

"The LORD appeared to him from afar, saying, "I have loved you with an everlasting love; Therefore I have drawn you with lovingkindness."

Jeremiah 31:3 NASB

Chapter Three

Parrot Talk

Can you remember the tales of pirates sailing on the seas in search of treasure and new lands? There are countless tails of their adventures and stories of longs days on tumbling waves. However, the success of the crew seemed to always include the crafty leadership of the ship's captain. You've heard their names: Captain Blackbeard, Captain Hook, and Captain Jack Sparrow. But who can forget the infamous Captain Long John Silver in the tales of Treasure Island and his trusted pet parrot, Captain Flint. Most images of Captain Silver include his brightly feather friend, perched on his shoulders. Parrots like Captain Flint were entertaining sidekicks for captains because of their constant and accurate mimicking of their captain's

44

words. These birds would often reiterate the commands of their captains, putting them on loop.

As fun as it was to hear the imitation of human words in a bird's voice, I believe we all have been exposed to a far less humorous parrot talk. I'm not talking about the cute, sing-song phrases from a multicolored bird. I am referring to our tendencies to repeat the words that have been spoken over us. That's how I've come to define *parrot talk*. It is our tendency to refer back to the words our original caretakers spoke concerning us (whether to us directly or about us) and accepting them as our personal truths. It is this tendency that causes us to put their words on loop, rather than our Shepherd's declaration of His real plan for us. Our proclivity to replay the words of the people who first had privy to our young, impressionable ears is due to principalities. Principalities, by their Greek definition, are the words and actions that presented themselves first in our lives, therefore being held with highest regard. Principalities are the words that our parents, caretakers, older siblings or whomever we looked to for love and acceptance as a child, spoke over us. Because we loved and trusted them, their words took priority in our minds. Now, if you were blessed to have very mature, intentional parents or caretakers, you heard words that affirmed your God-given gifts. You received reaffirming statements like: "you're special", "you're smart", or "you can do anything". Who can forget the award-winning quote from Viola Davis' character in the movie, *The Help*: "You is kind. You is smart. You is Important." That scene in the movie was a heart-touching moment where a loving caregiver realized the importance of speaking well over a child. Many of us were fortunate to have such people in our lives-people whose words were

> *Our proclivity to replay the words of the people who first had privy to our young, impressionable ears is due to principalities*

encouraging and motivating. However, naivety won't allow you to ignore the fact that many others did not hear such pleasantries. Many children hear much harsher sentiments of their lack of worth, value or ability. You've heard those parents in the grocery store line spew out non-retractable words to their children: "Get over here and quit showing out! You're acting just like your crazy daddy!" We never know the struggles of those parents or our own parents for that matter. So, let's not be so quick to point fingers. We aren't aware of the circumstances they were handed or the principalities they still hold in their ear gate. If this brings up bitter memories of the unkind words spoken to or about you, I pray you can offer forgiveness and grace to those who may have mishandled your beginning. And not just for your early caretakers, but all the voices you encountered along the way. There are others; classmates, teachers, first boyfriends or girlfriends, who had the ability to be the source of our principalities. It could be anyone who you held with high enough regard to allow their words to impact you. Principalities can be even more damaging in the relationships which we chose for ourselves. We hoped they'd whisper sweet nothings in our ears, but instead, they wounded us. It is those relationships that we often put on loop in our heads. It's those break-ups that leave us scared and guarded. After all, we couldn't choose our family members. God decided who they would be. But we did choose our last partner and that choice gave them access to our ears, heart and mind. That's why I believe the words or perceived words that are spoken during a romantic relationship can create the most squawking in *parrot talk.*

I hope by now you see that principalities can be powerful. They can be crippling and stunt your growth. They can be demeaning and debilitating. This is why I believe Paul pinned these words in Ephesians 6:12: "*For our struggle is not against flesh and blood, but against the rulers [principalities], against the powers, against the world forces of this darkness, against the spiritual [forces] of wickedness in the heavenly [places].*" Our greatest struggles aren't against people, but against the words they first spoke about us. It difficult to dismiss the voice in your head that keeps repeating the misinformation you were sold. *Parrot talk* is relentless in its pursuit to convince you that they were right. However, you must be just as determined to remind yourself that they did not consult God about you. Who else could know the original plan the Shepherd had for you when he placed you in your mother's womb?

Before I formed you in the womb I knew you, before you were born I set you apart; I appointed you as a prophet to the nations." Jeremiah 1:5 NIV

God knew you and His plan for you before you were even a thought of your parents. He designed you with a special purpose, and long before anyone else could even see your face, He was there whispering your destiny into your spirit. This is why it is imperative to learn the voice of your Shepherd. You're going to be on a treacherous journey called life, with principalities lurking around every corner. You will have to know what your Shepherd knew about you way before the world got access to your ear. I encourage you to relish this time on your Shepherd's shoulders as He tells you what He's known about you all along. Study what His Word says about you. Search where He calls you the "apple of His eye" (Deuteronomy 32:10) or how "He has loved you with an everlasting love"(Jeremiah 31:3)

If you need to hear His purpose for you, Jeremiah 33:3 instructs you to *"Call to Me and I will answer you, and I will tell you great and mighty things, which you do not know."* Did you hear that? There are great and mighty things He wants to accomplish in your life. You must simply ask Him and He will answer.

You must take a very intentional and active role to interrupt the parrot talk and listen to your Shepherd's voice. Hit the stop button on all the exes whose words or actions told you that you did not deserve to be loved. It's your responsibility to silence the rhetoric of "not enough", "unworthy", and "unlovable". Wrestle with those past voices until they lose their power. Once you hear what your Shepherd said about you in the womb, I encourage you to write it down. Place sticky notes or index cards that debunk your principalities and confirm your purpose.

Stick a cracker in that's parrot's beak and quiet his taunting.

ON THE SHOULDERS OF MY SHEPHERD

Chapter Four

Verbally Transmitted Diseases

Since your sixth grade year in school, I'm sure you've been inundated with information about the transmission of diseases from sexual contact with an infected person. STD education was probably an optional piece of your curriculum. They gave you pamphlets full of the different types of diseases and treatments. Your instructor probably showed you hideous, graphic photos of what a case of chlamydia looked like. If you're like me, I was scared to kiss until about the seventh grade! Don't worry. I am not about to force you to relive those horribly embarrassing moments in your sex ed classrooms. No, I'm about to introduce to you a far more deadly type of contact. I don't have any photographic evidence to prove how deadly this type of contact can be. There aren't any real physical symptoms that I can put in a slide show. No, these symptoms are the subtle ones that pop up in your relationships. These diseases are just as easily contracted, though. They can very easily spread with even limited exposure to any infected person. And like many STDs, these diseases can lay dormant inside of you for years without your knowledge until something triggers it or until you infect someone else. What disease could possibly be more lethal and less detectable that HIV, you ask? I want to school you on the detrimental disease that my Shepherd had to heal me from in the pastures after countless break-ups. It's called

> *Verbally transmitted diseases are the negative words of others that we have internalized and accepted as our personal truths and thus reenact them in our lives.*

verbally transmitted diseases. Verbally transmitted diseases are the negative words of others that we have internalized and accepted as our personal truths and thus reenact them in our lives. It's the hurtful names and comments of those we were once connected to that haunt us, even in subconscious ways, and have such a huge impact on how we view ourselves. There is nothing idiopathic about our current state. It all stems from what was spoken to or about us. Let's go back to our grocery store where we've observed parents speak ill of their children. I'm willing to bet you've also heard an adult refer to a child as "bad". It's those same kids who've been called "bad" all their lives who eventually believe it and become part of our criminal justice system. After you've heard something so long, you finally believe it! Have you been called "bad"? Or maybe unattractive. No, that wasn't it for you? How about a thug or trap queen? Maybe, just maybe, it wasn't even directly said to you but you perceived the message that all you would ever be good for was sex. It's those words that have transmitted into our souls and have infected us. Let's not bypass the role media has played in transmitting these diseases. Video vixens and hip-hop award shows have engrained a false sense of what's attractive in our minds. Social media has been instrumental in ensuring the latest images of sex, success and fame crowd your newsfeed. Paul would once again wave the red flag, warning you of the spiritual battle you're up against. It's important to address the words that were spoken about you (principalities) and even the subliminal messages you have received. If you fail to address the principalities in your life, you run the risk of falling into the life-altering trap of verbally transmitted diseases. I believe the wise Solomon would also jump in and recite a very well-known scripture:

"Power of life and death is in the tongue" Proverbs 18:21

There is so much power in what we speak that our Shepherd included this scripture in the Book of Wisdom. *Verbally transmitted diseases* will not only alter your life, but if you're not careful, they will indiscriminately

> **Verbally transmitted diseases will not only alter your life, but if you're not careful, they will indiscriminately infect other hosts**

infect other hosts. They will lay dormant in your mind and heart until the conditions are perfect to find another victim. The moment your new love makes you feel anywhere remotely like the last, you will lash out and infect him or her with hurtful words or even confusing silence. This is why time on the Shepherd's shoulders is so imperative to healthy relationships. If we don't allow Him to heal every verbal wound and affliction from our past, we will inevitably carry them into our future. Unknowingly, we will be the source of pain for another. Your healing from words are so important to your Shepherd. He desires you be whole and unaffected by the wounds of people who were themselves wounded. He wishes to erase the shame and guilt associated with being infected. He wants it desperately for you....even if it means private time with Him alone on His shoulders. Yes, I said the dreaded word, "alone". In order to be whole, your Shepherd may put you in isolation, in order to reduce being reinfected by others. You see, that's the part we singles hate, being alone. But if you're suffering from a verbally transmitted disease, you may need to be quarantined. There is a need for time alone with the only One who offers a healing balm. I get it. Loneliness will give us a false sense of urgency to jump into the next relationship. No one wants to be alone. Yet remember this, seasons of loneliness are temporary. They weren't meant to last forever. In these seasons, you must rely on His love for you and trust the healing process. Cakes can't rise in the oven if you open the door too soon. Clay can't be perfectly formed in rooms with too much vibration. You too, can't be made whole, if you keep allowing access from others into your life too soon. Sit still. Be soothed by His steady gate as you walk through the fields. Allow Him to replace all that was misspoken of you with his eternal thoughts of you.

ON THE SHOULDERS OF MY SHEPHERD

Chapter Five

Rejecting Misplaced Expectations

"All my life, I've been looking for, somebody else to make me

whole"-India Arie

The Disney Delusions

The scene opens like this: The forest was lovely and filled

with gorgeous, fragrant flowers and a babbling stream that flowed

through its center. The birds were singing hymns that stirred the

entire woods. Their song was cheerful and hummed the sentiments

of love. Even the squirrels, rabbits and the cranky old owl were

lulled by the melody. Suddenly, her voice accompanied the whistle

of the birds and a hypnotic ballad filled the air. It was the voice of

the beautiful maiden from the cottage. Her grace and beauty were matchless. Her presence was sheer enchantment and all the forest animals strolled with her through the woods as she sang with a voice of angels. The parade of fuzzy creatures, feathered friends and heavenly melodies filled the air and caught the attention of a visitor. The handsome prince was gallantly riding his royal steed through the forest for an afternoon stroll. The sound of her voice captured his curiosity and he was mesmerized. He followed the trail from her melodic notes until his eyes found her. Her flowing golden locks… her cheeks that would make rose petals envious…her lips sparkled with dew…and that voice…her voice. He was forced into a trance and knew he had stumbled upon the love of his life. He quietly snuck up behind her and joined in with her chorus: "I know you; I walked with you once upon a dream". They danced through the woods, singing and gazing into the eyes of their true love. "And I know it's true that visions are seldom all they seem. But if I know you, I know what you'll do. You'll love me at once, the way you did once upon a dream"...

And you know how it ends. They lived happily ever after.....

ON THE SHOULDERS OF MY SHEPHERD

Yep, you just felt it too. Your heart just swelled. The hopeful rush of magic, true love and fairytale endings just flooded you. And now you're singing the theme song of Disney's Sleeping Beauty. Don't feel guilty. We're all singing too.

Disney movies have that effect on us all. We each have spent hours and hours of laying on the carpet, while our eyes were glued to the love stories of gorgeous, flawless princesses who one day were swept up in the arms of strong, dapper princes. Every little girl has played in her mother's pearls and heels and dreamt of attending the ball. Each of us has fantasized about dancing until midnight in the arms of a dreamy Prince Charming. We have all waited for the day that a man would declare his undying love for us and battle dragons to rescue us. I'm willing to bet that every woman was once a girl who believed in true love's kiss. That's until far too many frogs failed to transform into princes, no matter what kind of lip gloss we wore. Yes ma'am. We've all been there. We all have fallen prey to the *Disney Delusions. Disney Delusions* taught us that in one magical moment, love would find us, dressed in a cape and crown. Our hearts would be instantly certain we had the one. He would feel the same. Birds would sing. The sun would shine. Angels were smiling from heaven. And love would last until the end of time. The end. As beautiful as those stories were, the reality is that they were just that-stories. As children, we were inundated with fairytales of Disney princesses and their enchanting lives of love and romance. We bought the storyline-hook, line and sinker. So we began many of our romantic relationship with the expectations of Princess Jasmine's happy ending. Our standards were constructed by scripted plots and characters. Even into adulthood, we carried the glimmer of hope that our childhood fantasies would one day manifest in a real life happily ever after.

So before you run into your daughters or niece's video library and burn every Disney DVD, let me stop you. Most of my favorite memories are those of watching those movies or pretending to be a princess. Even as a parent, my most memorable vacations was taking my son to the Magic Kingdom, where I found myself caught up in childlike laughter and giddiness all over again. I'm not anti-Disney. I believe they are wonderful, beloved stories and I probably own every single one. I simply want to point out the effect those movies had on our romantic expectations; especially if we were never presented with the reality of real love and the biblical truths that explain courtship and marriage. I am a fervent advocate of stirring up the imaginations of our children through reading and movies. I adore watching children play, creating imaginary worlds and portraying super powers. I would never suggest that children should not be allowed to be children, and explore the world through innocence and untainted wonder. That's the beauty of childhood. Christ even encourages us to recapture the faith we once had as children in Matthew 18:3: "And he said: "*Truly I tell you, unless you change and become like little children, you will never enter the kingdom of heaven.*" Don't stifle their childlike faith or yours for that matter. Please don't be mistaken. I'm not trying to strip you of your preadolescent fairytales; I just want a moment to sell you a better one.

> *What if I told you there was a far better love story than that of Cinderella or Snow White?*

What if I told you there was a far better love story than that of Cinderella or Snow White? What if I share with you that I've met a prince who won my heart and has romanced me over and over again? Would you share this story with your children if I could convince you that Disney could not even touch the love tale I encountered? Can I tell you about it?

Once upon a time, I was a filthy young woman; covered in dirt and bruises. My sense of worth was at an all-time low. I was clueless about who I was and the value of my life. Unaware of my true identity, I picked the wrong relationships. I simply chose the men who chose me. If they showed enough interest, I'd settle for less than I really wanted or deserved, because I was sure that I would never have what I really desired. After all, I had waited and looked long enough and he never showed up. So I became a habitual settler. I remained in substandard relationships way past their expiration dates. I made excuses for inexcusable behavior. I hid my relationship from family and friends to avoid eyes that would say that I could do better. I isolated myself. I was selective of the details I shared with my girlfriends. And year after year, relationship after relationship, I was buried deeper and deeper into worthlessness.

ON THE SHOULDERS OF MY SHEPHERD

However, one day while I was in a relationship sabbatical, I met my Love. He was such a gentleman. Unbeknownst to me, He had been watching me all along. He never pushed His way into my life. Never once, did He manipulate me or coerced me into a relationship. He just quietly, yet persistently pursued me. He understood the weakness of my nature and knew I could never rescue myself, so He selflessly exchanged His virtue for my wickedness...His strength for my helplessness...His immortality for my dying heart. He bargained with the Creator of Heaven to sacrifice His throne for an eternity with me. Before I even agreed to accept His hand, He endured indescribable pain and shame just to be able to call me His own. He courted me by leaving love notes and surprising me with gifts of sunshine and rainbows. When enemies pursued me, He never failed to protect me. All this, even before I said yes to Him. He had no guarantee that I would reciprocate His affections, but He kept coming after me. The times I was aimless and uninspired, He affirmed my gifts and value by giving me glimpses of my destiny. I'd pull away. He'd move closer. I'd act ridiculously shameful. He'd love harder. I'd hurt Him. He'd forgive me. I'd flaunt other men in front of him. He'd pursue harder. And when all else failed, He carried the weight of the cross up a hill and delivered Himself into the hands of accusers to prove His love for me. He gave His life there, on that same hill, so that we could be together forever. He even remained there three whole days just to seal the deal. With all my misinterpretations of real love, He became a living example for ultimate love, just for me. I have never seen this kind of love portrayed in any movie. I've only read about it once in a great Book. This is the love of Jesus. He embodied the greatest love story of all time. Not Disney. But a humble carpenter, who rescued me from myself and loved me until I learned how to love myself.

I wonder what would happen if we began to share this love story with our children. What if we taught our daughters that this is the way a man shows his love? What if we told our sons of what it truly means to love a woman

> *What if we did not depend on the writers of Disney to define what fairytale endings look like, but instead direct them to the Author of love?*

the way Christ loves the church? What if we did not depend on the writers of Disney to define what fairytale endings look like, but instead direct them to the Author of love? I believe that this is the love story that is worth broadcasting all over the nation. This is the most accurate depiction of what real love is…this is the proof that real love does exist...this is the template by which we should follow. There are no magic spells or fairy godmothers. There's only a Savior who desires to change our perspectives on love and relationships. There is only a Shepherd who wants to walk with you until you heal from all the misuse of l-o-v-e. Try a different story. Trust a new tale. Dream another dream.

ON THE SHOULDERS OF MY SHEPHERD

Chapter Six

The Performance Driven Life

Inevitably, by the time children reach middle school, they will begin to exhibit some rather stupid behavior. Please excuse the bluntness of my opening sentence, but I don't know any other way to describe it. Just plain stupid. Hormones overtake rational thinking and every word that comes out of their mouths seems utterly senseless. Don't laugh. You were once there too. You are guilty of the hormone-influenced, my-parents-don't-know-jack, but my-friends-are-geniuses, early teen years! It's in those adolescent years that we begin to be very concerned, almost consumed, with the opinions of our peers. Peer-pressure is at its all-time high during these formative years and every braces-wearing teen feels the weight of it. We have such an immense need to win the approval of those we deem important that we transform into actors on a stage and give Oscar-award performances to win their approval. We become performance driven.

Go to any local junior varsity or varsity football game and I'm willing to bet after a game winning play, the player is quickly looking to the sidelines to make sure his favorite cheerleaders has her pom-poms raised. And of course, those young ladies in the stands didn't wear those tights and cut-off tops for their girlfriends. No, they spent hours picking out that perfect outfit and primping just to get the attention of the boys at the concession stands. Now, it didn't start in middle school. Toddlers, just learning how to walk, learned how to take a few steps for the applause of doting parents. Conversely, it doesn't end there either. As adults, we spend a lot of time concerning ourselves with the opinions of others and performing for their approval. Don't get me wrong. We all love to hear, "good job", "well done" or "that was awesome". Just like children, we need positive reinforcement to encourage us to make good choices. The problem enters when the primary focus for our decisions are based on gaining applause, recognition or praise from people.

Becoming performance driven is an easy trap to fall into. After all, on our jobs, our raises are predicated upon our performance. In sports, the greatest performing athlete is paid the most. No matter where we look in our culture, we are conditioned to work for the praise of others. If your Instagram photos are catchy, you'll quickly gain thousands of followers. The highest ratings on television will place actors in Oscar nominations like lightning. I don't disagree wholly with the notion of being awarded for an outstanding

> *You should never tie your personal worth closely to the responses of other people*

performance. I want to point out the danger of deriving validation from applause. You should never tie your personal worth closely to the responses of other people. If there is one guarantee we all have in life, it is change. And just like the seasons and weather, people change. Their opinions of you will change. Their support of your vision will diminish. Their standing ovation can quickly transform into a walk-out if you choose a path that disinterests or offends them.

ON THE SHOULDERS OF MY SHEPHERD

The very same people you strove so hard to impress can become fascinated with the next best thing and turn their attention away from you. If your sense of value is dependent on their presence, you will find yourself on a never ending rollercoaster of people pleasing. Christian hip-hop star, Lecrae quoted it best, "If you live for people's acceptance, you will die from their rejection". When Paul was teaching to the church in Galatia, he was clear about the need to steer clear of performance driven proclivities. In Galatians 1:10 NIV, Paul warned,

"Am I now trying to win the approval of human beings, or of God? Or am I trying to please people? If I were still trying to please people, I would not be a servant of Christ.

In the pastures of our journey to becoming healed and whole, there will be deafening "bahhhh's" from all the other sheep. Yes, there are times where we feel led to perform by their noise. But it's our Shepherd who we must seek to please. It is his applause that we must crave. It is His "well done" that should create a hunger and thirst within us. The more our appetite increases for His satisfaction and glory, the more our lives expand, because we become less focused on others' approval and more driven to please God. In no way am I suggesting this it is easy to focus our eyes on our Shepherd rather than our fellow sheep. What you must be, however, is intentional.

Can I share with you a very intimate moment while my Shepherd was prodding me to write this section of the book? When I began to struggle with what to write about performance driven living, He forced me to be painfully honest with Him and myself. I was hitting multiple writing blocks and quickly loosing motivation for completing the manuscript. A series of personal setbacks and hardships were blocking my creative flow and I felt I couldn't clearly hear the direction He wanted me to go. He was healing me of my need to perform for others. I was sure of that. People-pleasing was slowly losing its grip on me and I could feel the freedom. But there was still this unexplainable weight I was feeling with every passing moment I neglected to write. I would force myself to write, but it was only a jumbled piece of mess. One day while fighting my funk, He led me to meet with a gifted mentor of mine. In her office, I began to share my current circumstances and how it was delaying my writing process. She asked me a pivotal question, "what are you most afraid of?" I paused and repeated the question again in my head. I breathed heavy and my heart sped up as I heard my voice respond, "I am afraid of disappointing God". "Afraid" did not adequately describe what I was feeling. I was all out terrified of God glancing at me from Heaven with disappointed eyes. I wanted Him to be pleased with this book. I was desperate for His smile with every sacrifice of time and typing. I would complete each chapter with childlike anticipation, "Daddy, did you see me? Did you see me? I did it. I finished another one..." I needed Him to be happy with the work of my hands. And it was this acknowledgement of my greatest fear that I realized I was in the midst of my greatest performance. I was yet again in performance driven mode, however this time, rather than focusing on people, I was trying to perform for my Shepherd.

I already hear your question- "What's wrong with trying to please God?" Nothing. Absolutely, nothing. Our aim should always be to live our lives for His glory. The problem enters when we begin to *perform* for Him. There's such a temptation to perform for Him because we have been conditioned to perform for people. We expect God to react similarly to people and applaud our work. However, the Bible warns us that God is not like man. While we were created in His image, our natural responses differ from His until we train ourselves how to have God-like responses. You don't have to pretend with God. You don't have to take grand measures to gain his love, attention or affection. It already belongs to you. God is already insanely in love with you. He has no need for you to put on an act. He already loves every inch of you! I had to realize that whether I completed this book or not, His love for me would not change.

"Who will separate us from the love of Christ? Will tribulation, or distress, or persecution, or famine, or nakedness, or peril, or sword?..... For I am convinced that neither death, nor life, nor angels, nor principalities, nor things present, nor things to come, nor powers, nor height, nor depth, nor any other created thing, will be able to separate us from the love of God, which is in Christ Jesus our Lord." Romans 8:35;38

There is no shortcoming that can separate you from His love. And there is no flawless performance that will cause Him to love you more. He has already proven His love through Christ Jesus. Here's your permission to take off the mask of being perfect for Him. Relieve yourself of the need to perform for His love. Allow yourself the freedom of transparency by coming before your Shepherd just the way you are. This requires an intentional shift in your thinking. It's difficult, I know, because religion has conditioned us to perform in

> *God's love is not predicated on what the church deems impressive*

church. Many church platforms have taught us that the more we dance or shout or the louder we sing and hoop, we will gain the attention or adoration of the saints. However, God's love is not predicated on what the church deems impressive. God is impressed with your gifts, your personality and entire person. Do you know why? Because *He* made you. He knows your entire story, from your conception to burial. He's seen your greatest accomplishments and also your lowest fall and He couldn't be more in love with you than He already is at this exact moment in time. Bask in that fact now!!! He's impressed, smitten, captured by you *right now*!!! Realizing His enormous love for me was not predicated on performance freed me. Do I still seek to please my Shepherd? Absolutely. But instead of trying to win His affection by dressing up in make-up and a costume, I am learning how to become righteous…the person I was originally intended to be. (We will discuss how to become righteous in a later chapter). The moment I grasped the width, height, length and breadth of His love for me, I began to enjoy our journey together.

The Trap of Comparison

Our tendency to be performance driven is further intensified by a sneaky little bandit called comparison. Yep, comparison. It's subtle and crafty and it causes so many of us to lose the joy and freedom of authenticity. Often times, we're so busy looking over our shoulder at others, admiring them, that we overlook our own uniqueness and value. When we are quicker to value the looks, gifts, qualities or lives of other people more so than our own, we neglect one very important declaration from God: *You are fearfully and wonderfully made*!!![Psalms 139:14]

That's right!! God made you in a way that compares to no one else on the earth. There's not even another thumb print that matches yours. He is smitten by *you,* and you have become consumed with other people. Why are you wasting your time trying to compare or compete with anyone when God is already in love with everything He created in you? If you read Psalms 139:15-18, there's is a beautiful love note from God about you:

> *"My frame was not hidden from you when I was made in the secret place,*
>
> *when I was woven together in the depths of the earth.*
>
> *Your eyes saw my unformed body;*
>
> *all the days ordained for me were written in your book*
>
> *before one of them came to be.*
>
> *How precious to me are your thoughts, God! How vast is the sum of them!*
>
> *Were I to count them, they would outnumber the grains of sand—*
>
> *when I awake, I am still with you." Psalms 139:15-18 NIV*

That made me smile. Those verses helped to remind me that I am incomparable. In His eyes, I am loved and He thinks of me always. He

Ask Him about what He wrote about you

took the time to write my entire life story with a unique pen and plot.

How special I must be to have my very own story, written by an infinitely creative God, who crafted every plot, twist, climax and happy ending. My story was not to be identical to anyone else. I can't waste precious time hoping my story will look like yours. And you can't waste any time wishing yours was like anyone else's. Ask Him about what He wrote about you. He would love to show you what He has planned for you. Don't be fooled into believing that He loves someone else more than you by wanting what they have. He is no respecter of person; He has something very special planned just for you. Stop comparing your life, whether your beginning or present circumstances, to that of others. You have no idea what they've had to endure to get to the point in life you're envious of.

The Social Media Incubator

Social media has become an incubation tank for the trap of comparison. It has created a stage of envy, jealously and dissatisfaction with our own lives. With the click of a mouse, we can peep into the windows of people all over the world who appear to have highly exciting lives. They appear to be prettier, fitter, richer, popular, more intelligent, sexier, and the list goes on. The more fabulous they appear to be or the "deeper" their posts sound lead them to gain more likes and followers and suddenly, we find ourselves caught up in comparison. Lest we forget, many of the photos are photo-shopped and filtered. Many of the post we read are fabricated and embellished. And the details of less than ideal days, circumstances, relationships, bank accounts and closets are carefully omitted to give illusions of perfect lives. Don't be fooled. Do you really think someone would air the truth about their breakup, foreclosure, bankruptcy or mistakes?

With the gaining popularity of social media outlets, we have to be more secure in who we are so that we are not caught up in comparison. I recommend taking close note of how too much time on social media affects your mood and attitude. When you begin to feel yourself being depressed or self-critical after browsing newsfeeds, it is a good indicator that you need a break from social media. Be intentional about stepping away and becoming more in touch with your own life. Don't get me wrong, social media is an excellent tool for marketing or keeping up with friends/family that aren't easily accessible. Just know where to draw the line and avoid being obsessed with the lives of others more so than the reality of the life your Shepherd is walking you into.

The Risk of Conforming

"Be ye not conformed to the patterns of this world, but be ye transformed by the renewing of your minds" Romans 12:2 NIV

Here comes a confession: I am a magazine junkie. I love to read magazines. Essence. Vogue. Ebony. Self. People. Cosmopolitan. Glamour. InStyle. You name it, I'll read it. I love to read the relationship advice columns and the beauty advice. I skim through the trending news and the healthy recipes. But when I get to the fashion trend articles, man oh man! I get this rush of excitement that I can't explain. I love looking at the photos of the latest fashion trends and hair styles. And if I'm not careful, I will quickly flip to the "Where to Buy" section at the back of the book to find out where to purchase those cute booties on page 96. Don't judge me. I bet there's a column that gets you excited too! In today's time, you don't even need magazines subscriptions to find the latest trends. The internet gives access to a plethora of websites for the latest, greatest *whatever* you're looking for.

Here comes a second confession: If my Shepherd had not pursued me to exclaim my worth and my unique contribution to the world, I would have let the contents of those articles define who I am. It sounds pretty extreme, I know. How could magazines and websites have the kind of power to determine who I become? Truth is they don't. But the power of suggestion through marketing tools and strategies can subtly influence who we *think* we should become. I am not a conspiracy theorist, however, I am acutely aware of the amount of influence advertisements and media have on the shaping of our society. They can suggest how we dress, relate, eat, sleep, travel, buy, spend, cope, *live*. There exist brilliant marketing experts who study what we spend our money on or where we spend our time, and they draft marketing campaigns to drive our habits. Celebrities can be more influential in what we consider societal norms. If we allow current trends of the world around us to be louder than the voice of our Shepherd, we discard the warning of Romans 12:2...we conform.

ON THE SHOULDERS OF MY SHEPHERD

Conformation is to use our society's standards as our relational guides rather than our Shepherd's leading. To conform to

> *Conformation is to use our society's standards as our relational guides rather than our Shepherd's leading*

the patterns of the world around us means we decide that the advice of Cosmopolitan yields better advice than the Word of God, so we'll opt on the "How to Blow His Mind" article rather than the scripture that says abstain from premarital sex (1 Corinthians 6:18-20). I'm not sure about you, but I've followed that advice a time or two. I'm guilty of listening to the advice of well-meaning, non-believing friends and ended up wounded. Using the counsel of family members or our astrology reading seems harmless. Yet I can bear witness to the injuries I have sustained from following the patterns of my environment rather than my Shepherd. It wasn't until I was burned way too many times that I realized His way was better. Better, not easier always, but better.

Since God was the original relationship maker, I decided to trust His counsel over anyone else's. This is not to say that God is not able to speak through people. This is where it becomes important to get wise, Godly counsel. Surround yourself with other Believers who will teach, encourage, pray for and hold you accountable to maintaining Godly relationships. Stay in fellowship with likeminded sheep who desire to see you whole and healthy, while they are seeking the same goal. Your temptation will be to choose the more appealing path: the glamourous love advice from reality TV, magazine articles or your Facebook newsfeed. But be encouraged by the latter promise in Romans 12:2, "*so that you may prove what the will of God is, that which is good and acceptable and perfect*". Learn your Shepherd's *good, acceptable and perfect* path for becoming whole and having healthy relationships.

Masking the Pain

Now, we are about to embark on a part of our journey on His shoulders that I know is uncomfortable and many would prefer to bypass it. However, my Shepherd showed me just how pivotal this topic is as we walk through the hillsides of healing. This topic is widely misunderstood, vastly ignored and pharmaceutically over-medicated. It's one that plaques millions at one point or another in their lifetime, yet half of those are terrified to admit it. I'm talking about depression. Depression can be defined as a mental illness associated with thoughts of sadness, despair, hopelessness and even physical symptoms, such as loss of sleep, appetite or desires. The National Alliance on Mental Illness (NAMI) reported that "Approximately 1 in 5 adults in the U.S.—43.8 million, or 18.5%—experiences mental illness in a given year". Mental illness has historically been stigmatized so much that many are unclear of its symptoms or unwilling to acknowledge its existence. Many have erroneously made depression synonymous with weakness. Again, our culture has conditioned us to pretend to be unaffected by emotions, especially as it relates to broken relationships. One of my favorite biblical characters is David. I love David, probably because I can closely relate to his flawed humanity. There are stories of his giant-slaying bravery and ones of his epic lapses in judgement, and yet God intimately refers to David as "man after His own heart" (Acts 13:22). God adored David; an unequivocal love for his heart and devotion to the ways of God. David's shortcomings were no match for God's love for him. And the same can be said about you. Even in David's moments of despair, God's heart still leaped for

David. In the 42 and 43 Psalms, we find David admit something that we find hard to fess up to: he was depressed.

> *"Why, my soul, are you downcast? Why so disturbed within*
> *me? Put your hope in God,*
> *for I will yet praise him, my Savior and my God. My soul is*
> *downcast within me;" Psalms 42:5-6 NIV*

David found himself in the middle of a season of depression. He had plenty reason to be in despair, trust me. David found himself hiding out far away from home, in the midst of unbelievers who had no problem mocking him and his God, overwhelmed by troubles and to top it off, God was seemingly taking His sweet time answering his prayer. If that's not a recipe for depression, I don't know what else is. You may find yourself there right now. You have long desired for a healthy, loving relationship and you have trusted God to bring *the one*. Those who know you've prayed for a mate have observed your single journey with eyes full of judgement and nagging questions: "When are you ever going to get married" or "Why are you asking God for a mate? You just need to lower your standards or you're never going to find anyone." You've earnestly prayed to God give you a "sign" if your current relationship was right or to send you the one person you'd be praying for. He is only silent. Now loneliness and frustration are your only companions. And here it comes: depression.

Here's where we can learn from the man who captured God's heart. David sensed the spirit of depression that had crept in the time lapse between the prayer and the promise. He didn't deny it existed. He didn't allow self-condemnation to ignore the disturbance of his emotions. He did what you and I must first be willing to do: he acknowledged his feelings. You need to know that life is hard, especially if you're doing it alone. Life will come to knock the wind out of you, without any warning or apology. Life will send your emotions in a whirlwind and at

> *Depression doesn't make you weak, it only makes you human*

times, you may find yourself feeling depressed. Depression doesn't make you weak, it only makes you human. Even the spiritual giant David was affected about it. You aren't exempt. However, you can, just like David, overcome it! When depression robs you of the expectancy you once had in God, you must remind yourself to consciously put your hope in *Him*. David commanded his soul to praise God, even in the midst of whatever he was dealing with. It was a very intentional action. It has to be that deliberate, otherwise, depression will engulf you until you can't escape it. If you are finding it difficult to push through depression alone, I encourage you to find help. While prayer and reading God's promises in His Word will help restore your ability to hear God in the midst of depression and the Holy Spirit will fulfill His role as your Comforter, there is absolutely nothing wrong with also seeking professional help. Please drop the stigma and shame of seeking a counselor, psychiatrist or psychologist. If you need counseling or even medication to help you conquer depression, get it! Hear me. God's love for you is not diminished and your faith in Him is not questioned when you seek counsel. If you need help through the season of depression, I challenge you to be brave enough to ask for what you need.

Intentionally praising God through depression takes practice and repetition, and even very seasoned saints, like David can at times succumb to the weight of trials, disappointments and the pressures of life. But just like David, if you acknowledge your emotions and give yourself permission to feel, you can then take the necessary steps to also acknowledge that God is with you and He will restore your hope and joy. If you can magnify His faithfulness and wisdom even when life has stuck its foot in your neck, I promise you He will show just how big He is. God will draw near you and give you the strength you need to trust Him until your prayers are answered.

"The LORD is near to the brokenhearted and saves those who are crushed in spirit." Psalms 43:18

Here's an invitation for you to remove the mask you've used to pretend you're unaffected about difficult circumstance. This is your chance to give up the façade of "I'm fine….everything's okay". Now is your opportunity to ask for the help you need to walk out of despair into wholeness. Muster up all the strength to be transparent about the places that have weakened you and stolen your peace. I can guarantee you that once you acquiesce and lay it all down, your Shepherd will come scoop you up onto His shoulders. His invitation to come to Him, all that are weary and heavy laden is real [Matthew 11:28]. He *will* give you rest.

ON THE SHOULDERS OF MY SHEPHERD

Chapter Seven

The Pursuit of Righteousness

It's dawn. It's that sacred time of the morning when the air has yet to be warmed by the light of the sun. This is my favorite time of day. It's this crisp morning air that ushers in new mercies. It's when the earth appears still, waiting for the commands of the Lord. This is the time of day when God displays his marvelous artistry and all the birds worship their Maker with hypnotic melodies. And on this dawning, you wake up to see your Shepherd still at your side. You peep over the side of the mountain- the place where you've traveled to on His shoulders. You look over and see all the dangerous terrain you survived because you were carried by a Master Guide. The sight of all the danger that could have taken your life makes your insides leap with praise for the grace which was given and led you safely to this side of the mountain. That's when your Shepherd gently nudges you, nodding toward the mountaintop, signaling that it's time to finish our journey. So you begin to stir, now fully awake, and mount His shoulders to begin this last leg of your journey. It's morning....

Knowing Your Purpose-Your Place of Righteousness

If you're anything like me, you've probably read many books on how to figure out your purpose. Maybe you have consulted your Pastor or taken assessments. Or quite possibly, you have taken courses to help assist you in finding what it is you were made to do. Many of us have reached a place in our lives where we have become desperate to seek out our purpose. There is an overwhelming sense of urgency to get it now. Trust this fact; God is ready for you to get it too. Yes, while you are hungry for your purpose, God is eager to walk you into it! Before you were even conceived, God had created an assignment especially for you. While in the womb of your mother, he placed unique gifts and personalities that would assist in accomplishing that purpose. Just at the right time, you began to gain a thirst for righteousness and your soul decided it would not settle for less than your original design.

Righteousness, as my Pastor Wendell Jones has taught us, means 'to be as you were originally intended to be'. To be righteous means that you match the blueprint that God designed when you were only an embryo in the womb. It was God's

> *Righteousness means 'to be as you were originally intended to be'*

original intent for your life before heartbreak and disappointments set you on another path. There is so much freedom in becoming who you were meant to be. I can attest to the liberty that comes when you get to stand in the place of righteousness and finally *"become who you were meant to be"*. There's an abundance of fulfillment, peace and joy that floods you when you know your purpose and begin to operate in it. That's why you hunger for it and that's why God is leading you into it. There's someone you're supposed to be…that's your purpose. And it doesn't stop there. God, in His infinite wisdom and intentionality, placed certain talents, preferences and gifts inside of you that align with your purpose. He designed you, complete with all you need to accomplish the thing(s) you were made to do. Sadly,

I believe Believers as a whole suffer from *righteousness deficiency*. Or at least that was the commentary of my life. I didn't really have low self-esteem…I had low righteousness awareness. I simply did not know who I was supposed to be.

The pursuit of righteousness does something so incredible, not only in your relationship with God, but also your relationship with yourself. As God leads you closer and closer to the man/woman you were intended to be, you begin to fall in love with that person. Righteousness and self-hatred can't live in the same soul. There's an explosion of self-love that begins to dispel the lies you believed about yourself and bathes you in self-acceptance, forgiveness and grace. While God reveals more and more of the real you, you begin to see more and more of Him inside yourself. Pursuing righteousness causes you to fall deeper and deeper in love with God and His creation of you.

Righteousness is more so important for those of you who desire Godly marriages. Once you have an understanding of why you were created, you will only want to attach yourself to others who are pursuing righteousness also. There's something about knowing your purpose that opens your eyes up and makes you selective about the connections you make. Righteousness ignites the Kingdom living inside of you, making you in tune with your Kingdom assignment. Your mind shifts and you only want to begin relationships with people (romantic interest, jobs, friends, churches, etc.) that are tied to your place of righteousness and your Kingdom. Becoming righteous allows you to understand the importance of partnership and the need to choose wisely when you enter relationships. That's why Matthew 6:33 say this, ***"But seek first his kingdom and his righteousness, and all these things will be given to you as well". NIV***

You must know your place of righteousness first before you can make the best choices for partners. There's such a need to be acutely aware of your own purpose and begin to walk in it, then everything else will be given also. A marriage that is

consummated by two Believers who know *who* they are and *what*

> *You must know your place of righteousness first before you can make the best choices for partners*

their assignments are creates *righteous love.*

A marriage that is consummated by two Believers who know *who* they are and *what* their assignments are creates *righteous love.*

So here's the million dollar question. How do I find my purpose or my place of righteousness? The answer is simply this: ask Him. That's it. Ask your Shepherd to reveal to you the reason He formed you in your mother's womb. There's no better person than your Maker to tell you the reasons why you were made. It sounds incredibly simple, I know. But it is indeed the only answer. Ask Him, ask Him, ask Him. He is faithful to bring you back to your original design. He promises. Allow your Shepherd to carry you into your place of righteousness and trust His leading. I can guarantee you He has more planned than you could have ever imagined....

"I'll show up and take care of you as I promised and bring you back home. I know what I'm doing. I have it all planned out—plans to take care of you, not abandon you, plans to give you the future you hope for." Jeremiah 29:10-11 MSG

Developing Your Gifts

Once you understand your purpose, you must then begin the hard work of developing your gifts. It becomes your responsibility to gain knowledge and understanding about how to fine tune your purpose and grow in your place of righteousness. Your purpose will become such a source of fuel for you that you will have the energy and passion necessary to get the things you need to develop your gifts. This may require reading books, finding a mentor, becoming an apprentice, volunteering or even going back to school. Developing your gifts is a very humbling part of your journey, yet absolutely necessary. It will require sacrifices of time, energy, money and even some relationships.

As you develop your gift, your light will attract people and opportunities to you. As exciting as that is, seek guidance from your Shepherd on making healthy choices that will only further develop the Kingdom inside of you.

ON THE SHOULDERS OF MY SHEPHERD

Epilogue

Today is the day. It's your first day off the shoulders of the One who so lovingly ushered you into wholeness. I know your legs are a bit wobbly. I understand the fear of standing on your own feet again. After all, you've been carried on His shoulders for some time, safe in His arms. Your first day back in the pasture with the other sheep may even frighten you. Be comforted by the fact that Your Shepherd is still there. He will always be at your side and will forever be your Guide. May you always remember the scent of Him. I pray you never forget the rhythm of your Shepherd's breathing. I hope in days to come, you will remanence on the sound of His voice. May the lessons He taught you about life, love and yourself remain in your quiver. May you be reminded of His grace, which was more than sufficient to heal every wound. It is my hope, as you close this book, that you have become more familiar with His voice and trust the places He leads you. May the intimacy of your time with Him assure you of His faithful love for you.

Thank you for the courage to pursue healing and wholeness. That's no small feat. You discarded fear and allowed room for vulnerability to be placed in His hands. I'm grateful for the time you sacrificed to read these pages. I pray there was a portion that allowed you a glimpse of the reasons I am in love with my Shepherd. I am indebted to Him for the ways He healed my brokenness. He captured my heart the day He picked up its broken pieces and mended them back together. I hope you can say the same. He taught me how to trust the path He laid before my feet. This is also my prayer for you. May your journey from here always lead you to righteousness…may it be exceedingly, abundantly above all you imagined…may it grant you the love you desire…and may His glory shine forever on your face.

Psalm 23

A psalm of David.

The Lord is my shepherd, I lack nothing.

He makes me lie down in green pastures,

he leads me beside quiet waters,

he refreshes my soul.

He guides me along the right paths

for his name's sake.

Even though I walk

through the darkest valley ,

I will fear no evil,

for you are with me;

your rod and your staff,

they comfort me.

You prepare a table before me

in the presence of my enemies.

You anoint my head with oil;

my cup overflows.

Surely your goodness and love will follow me

all the days of my life,

and I will dwell in the house of the Lord

forever.

ON THE SHOULDERS OF MY SHEPHERD

Acknowledgements

When I was typing the final pages of this book, I high-fived God and grinned at him, exclaiming, "Daddy you are incredible. You blow my mind!!!" It's Him I have to acknowledge first. He wrote this book. He inspired every word. He led every chapter title and every concluding sentence. For that reason, I will bless [acknowledge] Him at all times (Psalm 34:1). Daddy, I can't thank you enough for loving me through to wholeness. Thank you for your persistence and compassion. Thank you for Wisdom, which knew the perfect path for my healing. I could not have had even the courage to trust you if You had not shown Yourself to be so faithful and loving. You have amazed me on this journey. You have given me more and more reasons to adore you. Your guidance has been my best, most reliable friend. Your voice is one I love to hear. Thank you for teaching me to hear you.

ON THE SHOULDERS OF MY SHEPHERD

To the two people who birthed me and loved me in so many ways I can no longer count. Billy and Barbara Martin, you two are incredible. You are my greatest and loudest supporters. You prayed for me, even when I was unaware. You introduced me to the best gift ever-Jesus. I will always be indebted to God for placing me in your care. I'm so grateful to belong to you. You have never failed to show up to every event of my life, and that's no small thing. To say I'm grateful is an understatement. I really can't find the words to express just how much I love you.

To my brother and best friend, thank you for your consistent support. You have been there ever since I can remember and I can't thank enough for always joining me on life's adventure. To his wife Erica and their daughters, Ava and Layla, you two are Auntie's heartbeats. May you know life and love to the fullest. To my sister Patricia, thank you for being my ear during my first heartbreaks and love lessons. I will always remember that.

To all of my family…what did I do to deserve you? You people ROCK!!! I am amazed by your love. You have inspired me to maintain your traditions of love. Thank you for such a beautiful example. Your conversations, your prayers, your meals, laughter and dancing have shaped so much of my life.

To the man whose teaching inspire much of this book and has changed my life in ways I could not have ever imagined… my spiritual father and Pastor Wendell Jones. Thank you for your passion to push your sheep toward their purpose. To Pastor Jones, First Lady Nita Jones and the entire Changing Your Mind Ministries family, thank you for loving me to righteousness. Your love, support, prayers and encouragement has meant the world to me.

I have to thank my best friends (Jan, Tonya, Debra, Yxsumi) and my Sistah Girlz. It means so much to have girlfriends, standing behind you. Thank you for being behind me every time I turn around. Your friendship had made my life richer. To Rod Dogan who pushed me all the way to publication, thank you sir. To my mentors and QueenEssential 31 mentors, thank you for your prayers and counsel. I pray to be a better woman, mother and wife because of your teaching. A very special thanks to Mrs. Tanika Dillard: Wonder Woman Extraordinaire. Your mentorship, guidance and encouragement made this book come alive. I love you ma'am!

Dr. Paul Thompson, you sir are the reason my life shifted. Thank you for the words of encouragement you spoke to me. I will always be grateful for the book you placed in my hands and your belief in me. Vivian McWhorter-Hubbard, thank you for diligence and faithfulness in editing this book.

Certainly not least, I saved my most favorite person for last. Elijah, your mommy is so captivated by you. You are such a brilliant and loving boy. Your heart has blown me away! I love how you love people and practice kindness, compassion and goodness. You gave me so many reasons to pursue abundant life. Your life was exactly what I needed to go after God. I could not be more honored than to be your mother. May you know that you are loved immensely and unconditionally. Trust that nothing is impossible for you if you believe. May you walk out your purpose, all while holding God's hand. I love you.

ON THE SHOULDERS OF MY SHEPHERD

About the Author

Amaris L. Martin

…is a native of Seneca, South Carolina. She currently resides in Simpsonville, SC. She is called "mom", by a son she adores, named Elijah. She is called daughter by her parents, Billy and Barbara Martin, whom she credits as being her first examples of the love and commandments of God. She is called sister, Auntie, and a girlfriend to many others. But the name she prefers to be called is simply a servant of God. It is Amaris' desire to serve the people of God, wholeheartedly, following the example of Christ.

"Whosoever desires to become great among you, let him be your servant; just as the Son of Man did not come to be served, but to serve…"Matthew 20:26,28

She has a fervent passion for encouraging women through the Word of God, believing that through the blood of Jesus, we have been given the opportunity for an abundant, satisfying life. Through this belief, she became the founder of Queendom Come Coaching. Queendom Come Coaching is designed to teach and minister to women on how to be aware of their righteousness (to be as God's original design for their lives) position and how to develop the Queendom within them. It represents the sacred place God has given each of His daughter's to rule: her Queendom. Queendom Come Coaching embodies strength, dignity, righteousness, feminine power, gentleness, Godly principle, wisdom, and love. Amaris passionately teaches women to know that God desires to transform their lives into "a crown of glory".

"You will be a crown of splendor in the Lord's hand, a royal diadem in the hand of your God." Isaiah 62:3

For contact information, find her at www.queendomcomecoaching.com.

QUEENDOM COME

COACHING

ON THE SHOULDERS OF MY SHEPHERD

www.ingramcontent.com/pod-product-compliance
Lightning Source LLC
Chambersburg PA
CBHW020945090426
42736CB00010B/1266